Journey Through
The Sun

Reagan Miller

Crabtree Publishing Company

www.crabtreebooks.com

Dedicated by Reagan Miller
For my beautiful niece, Bryley Ocampo Miller—You are our ray of sunshine!

Author: Reagan Miller

Publishing plan research and development:
Sean Charlebois, Reagan Miller
Crabtree Publishing Company

Project development: Clarity Content Services

Project management: Clarity Content Services

Editors: Kristi Lindsay, Wendy Scavuzzo

Copy editor: Dimitra Chronopoulos

Proofreader: Kathy Middleton

Design: First Image

Cover design: Samara Parent

Photo research: Linda Tanaka

Production coordinator: Ken Wright

Prepress technician: Ken Wright

Print coordinator: Katherine Berti

Photographs:
NASA: p 7 lower, 8, 9; NASA/Goddard
Space Flight Center Scientific Visualization:
p. 6; StudioiStockphoto/ Thinkstock: p4; vovan/
shutterstock: p5; Stockbyte/Thinkstock: p7; Ralf
Juergen Kraft/shutterstock: p10; Anteromite/
shutterstock: p11; iStockphoto/ Thinkstock: p12;
Jochen Kost/shutterstock: p13; Jupiterimages/
Thinkstock: p14-15; Ant Clausen/shutterstock: p16;
JPL/Caltech/NASA: p17; left Brykaylo Yuriy/
shutterstock, Galyna Andrushko/shutterstock: p18;
Hemera/Thinkstock: p19; razihusin/shutterstock:
p20; Tatiana Popova/shutterstock: p21; Pieterpater/
shutterstock: p22; PRIMA/shutterstock:
background; Thinkstock: back cover; almagami/
shutterstock: front cover (girl); Milosz Aniol/
shutterstock: front cover (background)

Library and Archives Canada Cataloguing in Publication

Miller, Reagan
The sun / Reagan Miller.

(Journey through space)
Includes index.
Issued also in electronic format.
ISBN 978-0-7787-5309-4 (bound).--ISBN 978-0-7787-5314-8 (pbk.)

1. Sun--Juvenile literature. I. Title. II. Series: Journey through
space (St. Catharines, Ont.)

QB521.5.M54 2012   j523.7   C2012-901240-8

Library of Congress Cataloging-in-Publication Data

Miller, Reagan.
The Sun / Reagan Miller.
p. cm. -- (Journey through space)
Includes index.
Audience: Grades K-3.
ISBN 978-0-7787-5309-4 (library binding : alk. paper)
-- ISBN 978-0-7787-5314-8 (pbk. : alk. paper) -- ISBN 978-1-4271-8835-9
(electronic pdf.) -- ISBN 978-1-4271-9738-2 (electronic html.)
1. Sun--Juvenile literature. I. Title.
 QB521.5.A345 2007
523.7--dc23
                    2012006453

Crabtree Publishing Company

www.crabtreebooks.com   1-800-387-7650

Printed in Canada/102017/BF20170919

Published in Canada
Crabtree Publishing
616 Welland Ave.
St. Catharines, Ontario
L2M 5V6

Published in the United States
Crabtree Publishing
PMB 59051
350 Fifth Avenue, 59th Floor
New York, New York 10118

Published in the United Kingdom
Crabtree Publishing
Maritime House
Basin Road North, Hove
BN41 1WR

Published in Australia
Crabtree Publishing
3 Charles Street
Coburg North
VIC 3058

Contents

What Is the Sun?

We have all seen that the night sky is filled with tiny, shining **stars**. But did you know that there is one star that we can see during the day? That star is our Sun! Like most stars, the Sun is a ball of hot, glowing gases. The Sun is the closest star to Earth. This is why it looks bigger and brighter than other stars. The Sun shines so brightly in our sky, that we cannot see the other stars during the day.

Twinkle, Twinkle, Great Big Stars!

The Sun is one of billions of stars in the sky. The Sun is a yellow dwarf star. This means it is a medium-size star. Some stars are much larger and other stars are much smaller.

The Sun is also a medium-bright star. Stars give off different colors of light. The hottest stars are blue-white. The coolest stars are red-orange. The medium-hot stars are yellow. The Sun is a yellow star.

The Sun

Hot Stuff!

The Sun is not solid like Earth. It is made up of gases. The Sun has many layers. The **core**, or center, of the Sun is the hottest part. The Sun's light and heat are made in its core. The outer layer of the Sun is about 50 times hotter than boiling water!

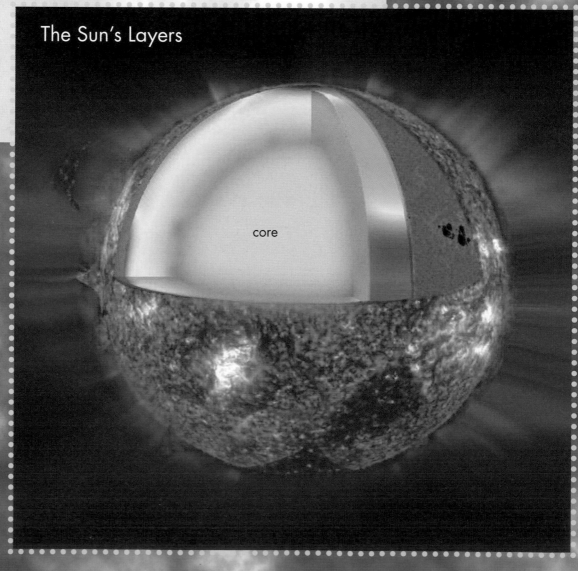

The Sun's Layers

core

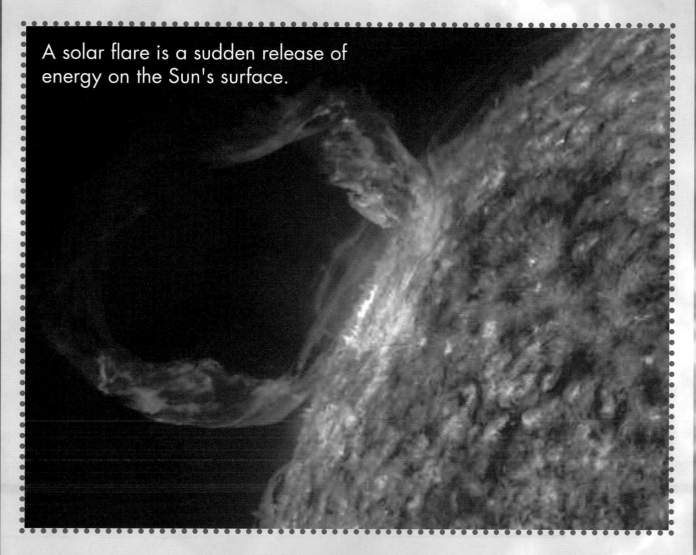

A solar flare is a sudden release of energy on the Sun's surface.

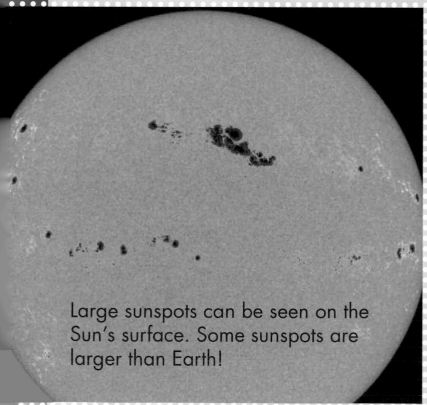

Large sunspots can be seen on the Sun's surface. Some sunspots are larger than Earth!

Seeing Spots!

There are dark areas called **sunspots** on the outer layer of the Sun. Sunspots are darker than the rest of the Sun. The temperature is cooler in these areas. **Solar flares** are sudden bursts of burning gases. Solar flares often happen near sunspots.

At the Center of It All

The Sun is the star at the center of our **solar system**. The solar system is made up of the Sun, the planets, moons, and other objects in space. All of the planets in our solar system **orbit** the Sun. To orbit means to travel in a path around an object in space.

Planets closer to the Sun get more of the Sun's heat than planets that are farther away.

Sun

Earth

Nearly one million planets the size of Earth could fit inside the Sun!

Supersized Sun!

The Sun is the largest object in the solar system. The Sun's huge size gives it strong **gravity**. Gravity is a force that pulls objects together. The Sun's gravity keeps the planets traveling in their paths around the Sun.

The Sun and Earth

The Sun is important for life on Earth. It gives us light so we can see. The Sun also gives us heat that warms the land, air, and water. Without the Sun's light and heat, Earth would be dark and cold. There would be no life on Earth without the Sun.

Plants need the Sun's light to grow.

If an airplane could travel to the Sun, it would take more than 26 years to reach it!

Perfect Position

The Sun is about 93 million miles (150 million kilometers) away from Earth. This distance is just right for life on our planet. The planets closer to the Sun are too hot for living things. The planets farther away are too cold.

Day and Night

Earth **rotates**, or spins, as it orbits the Sun. Earth spins on an **axis**. Earth's axis is an imaginary line through the middle of Earth from its top to its bottom. It takes 24 hours, or one day, for Earth to make one complete rotation on its axis. As Earth rotates, part of it faces the Sun. It is day in that part of the world. At the same time, the other part of Earth faces away from the Sun. It is night in that part of the world. As Earth rotates, it causes a **pattern** of day and night. A pattern is something that repeats.

When we are on the side of Earth facing the Sun, is it day or night?

night   day   Sun

Earth

When it is day where you live, it is night on the other side of Earth.

Does the Sun Rise and Set?

During the day, we see the Sun in different places in the sky. The Sun appears to rise in the morning, move across the sky during the day, and set in the evening. It is Earth, however, that is moving, not the Sun! The Sun appears to move across the sky because Earth rotates.

When our part of Earth is rotating toward the Sun, it looks to us like the Sun is rising. When our part of Earth is rotating away from the Sun, it looks to us like the Sun is setting. In the middle of the day, the Sun is right above our heads.

Why There Are Seasons

It takes Earth one year to orbit once around the Sun. Earth tilts, or leans, as it travels around the Sun. Earth's tilt is why there are seasons! The part of Earth that tilts toward the Sun gets more of the Sun's heat and light. There are more daylight hours there, so the Sun has more time to heat Earth and raise the temperature. In this part of Earth, it is summer. In the part of Earth that tilts away from the Sun, it is winter. Here, there are fewer daylight hours, less sunlight, and less heat. The temperature is colder. As Earth rotates, the seasons change from spring to summer to fall to winter.

Spring The top part of Earth begins to tilt toward the Sun. Temperatures get warmer. Days become longer than nights.

Summer The top part of Earth tilts toward the Sun. Temperatures are hot. Days are longer than nights.

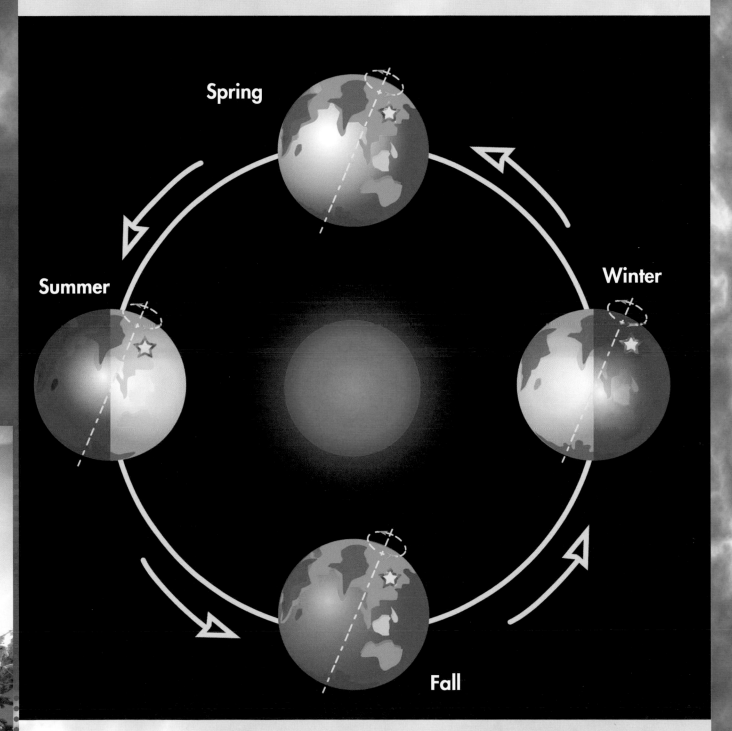

Fall The top part of Earth begins to tilt away from the Sun. Temperatures get cooler. Days become shorter than nights.

Winter The top part of Earth tilts away from the Sun. Temperatures are cold. Days are shorter than nights.

Solar Eclipses

A solar **eclipse** occurs when the Moon passes between the Sun and Earth. The Moon blocks some or all of the Sun's light from reaching parts of Earth. This causes the Moon to make a shadow on part of Earth. People on Earth in the Moon's shadow can see the solar eclipse. Those who are outside the Moon's shadow cannot see the eclipse.

Sun

Moon

Earth

This is how the Sun looks during a solar eclipse. It is not safe to look straight at the Sun, even during an eclipse.

ACTIVITY: Where Does the Sun Go at Night?

What You Will Need
- a flashlight
- a friend

Steps
Step 1: Stand 10 steps away from your friend.

Step 2: Shine the flashlight on your friend's stomach. The flashlight is the Sun. Your friend is Earth.

Step 3: Have your friend slowly rotate in one spot. Where does the light shine as your friend turns?

What Happens?
What pattern is made as your friend rotates?

How does this activity help you understand why we cannot see the Sun at night?

Learning More

WEBSITES

www.nasakids.com
Visit NASA Kids' Club for challenging space games and to learn about the latest information about space.

http://starchild.gsfc.nasa.gov/docs/StarChild/ StarChild.html
StarChild is a learning center for young astronomers.

Created by NASA, this website offers exciting images and activities.

www.kidsastronomy.com/astroskymap/solar-eclipse.html
This website has an interactive simulation of a solar eclipse.

OTHER BOOKS IN THIS SERIES
The Stars
The Planets
The Moon

Glossary

axis (AK-sihs) An imaginary straight line around which an object spins

core (kohr) The innermost layer or center

eclipse (ih-KLIHPS) When one space object partly or completely hides another space object

gravity (GRA-vih-tee) The force of attraction between matter

orbit (OR-bit) To travel around another object in a single path in space

pattern A set of events that is repeated

rotates To turn about a center point or an axis

solar flares (SOH-lur FLEHRZ) Sudden explosions of energy from the Sun's outer layer

solar system (SOH-lur SIS-tum) The system made up of our Sun, the eight planets, moons, and other space objects

stars Objects in space made of hot, glowing gases

sunspots (SUN-spahts) Dark, cooler areas on the outer layer of the Sun

Index